# *A Book About Your* Skeleton

**by RUTH BELOV GROSS**     **Pictures by DEBORAH ROBISON**

SCHOLASTIC INC.
New York Toronto London Auckland Sydney

*For Irving Sarnoff, M.D.*
*—for his many kinds of help*

Special thanks to Bernard Ghelman, M.D., Department
of Radiology, Hospital for Special Surgery, New York
City, for reviewing the manuscript for this book.

ISBN 0-590-30346-5

12                                                                              8 9/8 0/9

# A Book About Your Skeleton

Everybody has bones.

Everybody needs them.

If you didn't have any bones,

you would flop around like spaghetti.

Your bones are hard and stiff.

The rest of you is soft.

The hard, stiff bones help hold the soft part up.

And they give the soft part a shape.

You can feel the hard, stiff bones
that help hold you up
and give your body its shape.

You have more than 200 bones in your body —
long bones, short bones, flat bones, curved bones,
little bones, big bones.

There are bones in your head
and bones in your toes
and bones almost everywhere else in between.

All of your bones put together are your skeleton.

But a skeleton isn't just a pile of bones.
This isn't a skeleton.

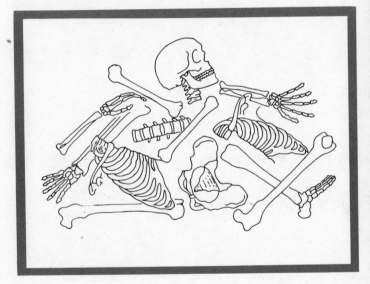

Neither is this.

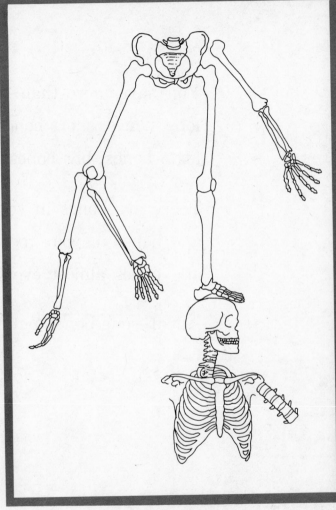

8

The bones have to be put together right!

It's a good thing that bones are hard.

If you bumped your head,

you might get a headache.

But the soft squashy brain inside your head

would be safe.

Your head bones are like a hard hat.

They keep your brain from getting hurt.

The bones in your head are your skull bones.
Construction workers have to be extra careful.
So they wear hard hats over their hard skulls.

11

Your heart and lungs are soft and squashy too,
but nothing will happen to them —
even when somebody hugs you too tight.
The bones that curve around your chest
keep your heart and lungs from getting hurt.

The bones that curve around your chest
are your ribs. You can feel them under your skin.
Maybe you can even count them.

Every bone in your body
is joined to at least one other bone.

Put your thumb and first finger together.
Can you see where your fingers bend?
The bending places are where two bones are joined.
The bending places are joints.

Strong, stretchy bands, like big rubber bands,
hold the bones together.
These bands are called ligaments.

Without the joints in your fingers,
your fingers would stick straight out.
You could never play ball
or play the piano
or button your buttons
or peel a banana.

Shoulders, elbows, and wrists are joints.

So are hips and ankles and knees.

How many things can you think of

that these joints help you do?

Other joints in other parts of your body
also help you move.

You can twist and turn
and touch your toes
because you have joints in your backbone.
Your backbone is made of many little bones
called vertebrae.

Another name for backbone is spine.

You can open and close your mouth
because you have two important joints
in your skull.

There are other places in your skull
where bones are joined —
but these joints do not move.

Can you feel the joints
on each side of your jaw
that let you open your mouth?

19

Your bones help you move.
And your joints help you move.
But you couldn't move — you couldn't
even stand — if you didn't have
muscles too.

Your muscles make your bones move.
The muscles are attached to your bones.
They pull on the bones to move them.

It takes many muscles just to take one step
— or to wiggle one of your toes.

Your skeleton began growing before you were born.

It wasn't hard and bony then.

It was made of soft, rubbery cartilage.

If you want to know what cartilage feels like,

pinch the end of your nose, or bend your ear.

Bit by bit, your skeleton got a little harder.

Bone was beginning to take the place of

the soft cartilage.

After you were born, your bones

kept on getting harder.

There was less and less cartilage in them.

**This baby's bones
are still soft and rubbery.**

Your bones are getting harder all the time.

And they are getting bigger too.

Your growing bones

are helping to make you bigger and taller.

They will keep on growing until

bone has replaced almost all of the cartilage.

Even an adult has some cartilage —

at the ends of some bones, in the ears and

nose, and in a few other places.

Some of the things you eat
help your growing bones get harder and stronger.

How tall will you be when you stop growing?
That's hard to say.
The bones in your legs may keep on growing
and making you taller
until you are 18 or 20 years old.

Your arm bones will stop growing at about
the same time as your leg bones.

But your hands and your feet may grow
for another year or two,
until you are about 21 years old.
A few other bones will still be growing
until you are 24 or 25 years old.

When your bones are fully grown,
they will be stronger than granite rock.
But even though bones are strong,
bones can break.

What happens if you break a bone in your leg?
The doctor puts the broken parts together,
and you get a plaster cast to wear.
You can ask your friends to sign the cast.
Then you wait for the bone to heal.

The cast keeps the broken bone
from jiggling around.
The bone will mend itself.

An X-ray picture will show the doctor
how well the bone is healing.

No matter how big or how small a bone is,
and no matter how it is shaped,
there are spaces inside the bone.

The big, long bones in your arms and your legs
have big, long spaces inside them.
And at the ends of these bones there are tiny spaces,
like the spaces in a sponge.
Other bones have tiny spaces too.

The spaces are filled with a mushy material
called bone marrow.
Red bone marrow is where blood cells are made.

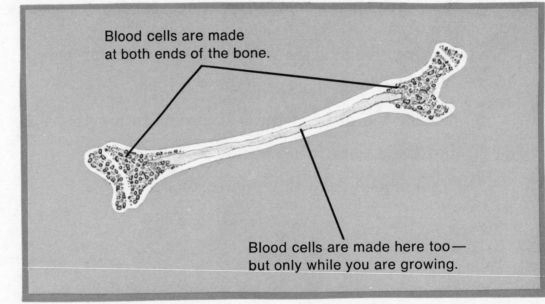

Blood cells are made
at both ends of the bone.

This is what
the inside of
a leg bone
looks like.

Blood cells are made here too—
but only while you are growing.

So your bones do more than hold you up
and help you move
and give your body a shape
and protect your squashy insides.
Your bones also help make your blood.

There are 206 bones in a human skeleton.
Every bone has a name.

In a real skeleton, the bones are white.
The bones in the picture, though, have different colors,
to make it easier to tell them apart.

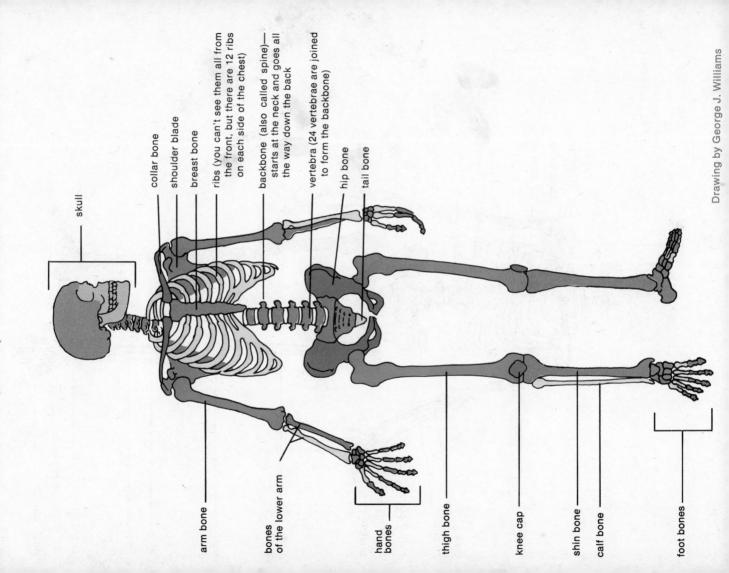

skull

collar bone

shoulder blade

breast bone

ribs (you can't see them all from the front, but there are 12 ribs on each side of the chest)

backbone (also called spine)—starts at the neck and goes all the way down the back

vertebra (24 vertebrae are joined to form the backbone)

hip bone

tail bone

arm bone

bones of the lower arm

hand bones

thigh bone

knee cap

shin bone

calf bone

foot bones

Drawing by George J. Williams

These are the same bones with their scientific names.

skull (made up of 8 bones in the cranium and 14 bones in the face)

cranium

clavicle

scapula

sternum

costae

spinal column (also called vertebral column)

vertebra

innominate bone

sacrum

coccyx

humerus

ulna

radius

carpal bones

metacarpal bones

phalanges

femur

patella

tibia

fibula

tarsal bones

metatarsal bones

phalanges